THE LADYBIRD

a·b·c

with illustrations by
G. W. ROBINSON

Publishers: Wills & Hepworth Ltd., Loughborough
First published 1962   ©   Printed in England

a

apple

b

balloon

C

cake

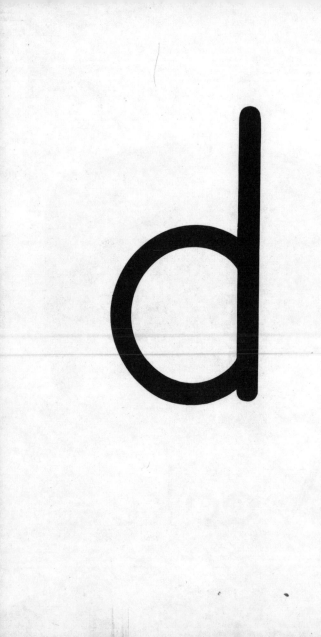

duck

e

elephant

f

fish

g

gate

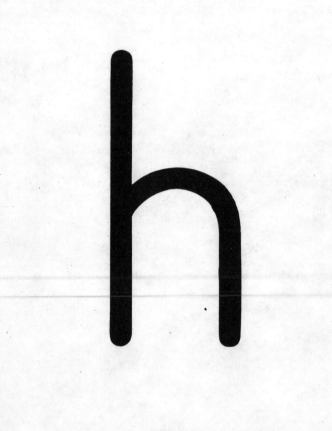

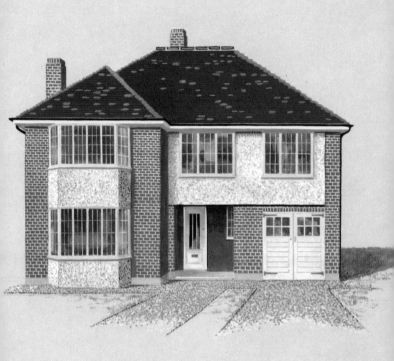

house

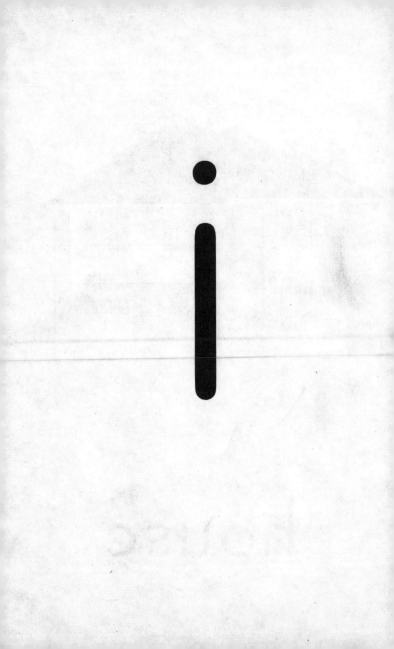

ink

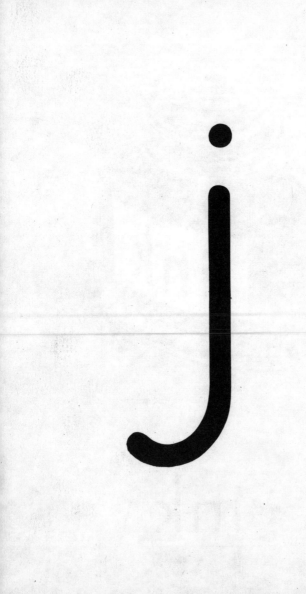

jug

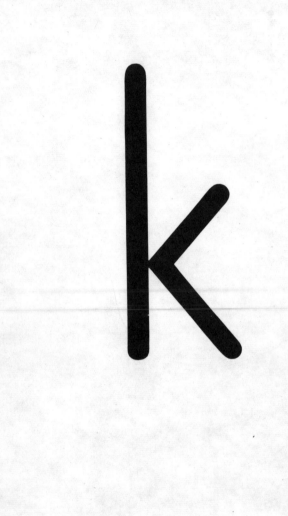

kettle

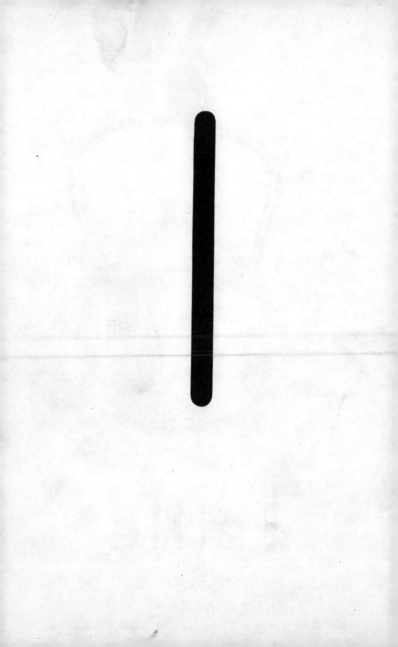

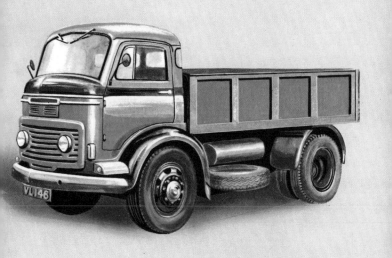

lorry

m

mice

n

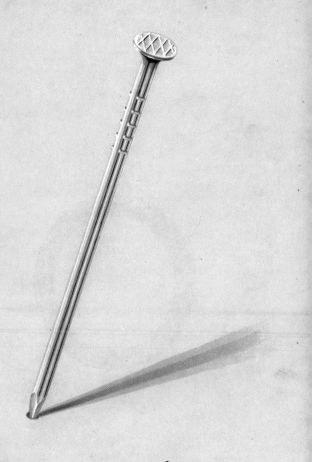

nail

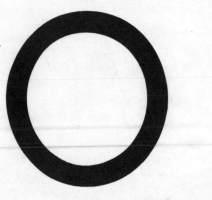

orange

p

postman

q

queen

r

rabbit

S

spoon

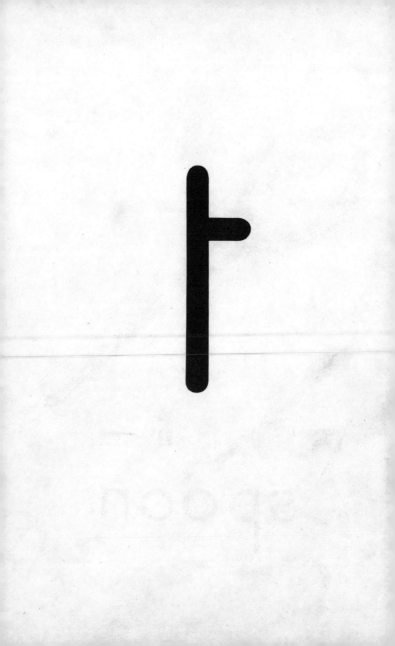

table

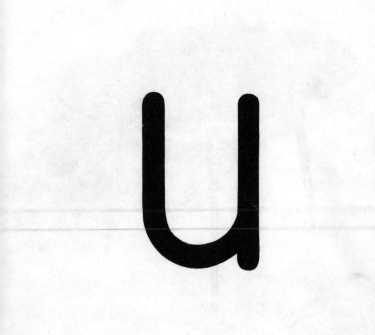

umbrella

V

van

W

window

x

y

yellow

Z

zebra